LET THERE BE FORGIVENESS

LET THERE BE FORGIVENESS

Gillian Stokes

MQP

MQ Publications Limited
12 The Ivories, 6–8 Northampton Street, London N1 2HY
Tel: +44 (0) 20 7359 2244 Fax: +44 (0) 20 7359 1616
email: mail@mqpublications.com
www.mqpublications.com

ISBN: 1-84072-975-9

1 3 5 7 9 0 8 6 4 2

Printed and bound in China.

CONTENTS

INTRODUCTION

WHAT IS FORGIVENESS? FORGIVENESS BENEFITS everyone it touches, healing pain and anger, and bringing about peace and a transforming wisdom. It's a skill that requires compassion, commitment, and effort; self-understanding, and a genuine desire to make amends. But anyone can learn it. Most importantly, forgiveness lies at the heart of Christianity.

"Forgiveness: To stop feeling angry or resentful toward someone for an offence, flaw, or mistake."
NEW OXFORD ENGLISH DICTIONARY (1998)

WE HAVE ALL ACTED BADLY AT TIMES. WHO, GIVEN a choice between honorable or dishonorable behavior, hasn't chosen the latter occasionally? It's human nature. But forgiveness is always available. We are surrounded by and constantly immersed in God's love, though we may choose to turn our faces away from it, caught up by sad events or a busy life. We can choose to turn back to the light and His forgiveness at any time. Our Father is always waiting.

TODAY IS A GOOD DAY TO START ACQUIRING THE art of forgiveness. The path might take some of us many years of slowly realized faith; for others, it may be achieved in a moment. In this book you will find practical strategies and inspirational thoughts to help you along your journey.

"If we confess our sins, he is faithful and just to forgive us our sins, and to cleanse us from all unrighteousness."

1 JOHN 1:9

PART 1

Why Forgive?

BEFORE HIS ARREST, TRIAL, AND crucifixion, Jesus gathers together his disciples for their last supper together. As he pours wine into each glass, he tells them the wine symbolically represents his blood, the blood that will be shed on behalf of all mankind as a willing sacrifice to absolve our sins. This new covenant, a contract willingly entered into for our sakes, is at the core of Christian forgiveness.

"This is my blood of the new covenant, which is poured out for many for the forgiveness of sins."

THE GOSPEL OF ST. MATTHEW 26:28

CHRISTIAN FORGIVENESS

FORGIVENESS IS AT THE HEART OF CHRISTIAN theology. Jesus died to redeem (forgive) our sins. The gospels describe how Christ forgave his persecutors even as he suffered the physical agony of crucifixion. In uttering His last words before death, "It is finished," Christ acknowledged the fulfilment of ancient prophecies and the culmination of His work on earth: "For this reason I was born, and for this I came into the world, to testify to the truth." (John 18:37). In willingly sacrificing himself and surrendering His spirit back to God the Father, Christ paid for the sins of the world.

FORGIVE US OUR TRESPASSES

MANY OF US HAVE RECITED THE LORD'S PRAYER since childhood. But have you ever really considered those familiar words? Jesus tells us that the forgiveness we seek is conditional on the fact that we already forgive those who, we feel, let us down. Forgiveness is not available by petitioning God if we still nurse any grievances against others. We shall be forgiven only when we can honestly say we have found it in our hearts to forgive—"Let he who is without sin cast the first stone."

"... and forgive us our trespasses,
as we forgive those who have
trespassed against us..."

THE GOSPEL OF ST. MATTHEW 6:12

UNLESS WE ARE CAPABLE OF PUTTING OURSELVES in the shoes of the person we believe has wronged us, with a heart filled with compassionate understanding and forgiveness, we cannot begin to petition for forgiveness ourselves. At another time, in another place might not that sinner as easily have been you? If you suspect so, it may be a little easier to extend sympathy and forgiveness. A heart that is closed to forgiveness remains closed to love. And if we stay forever closed to love, we will never know the unconditional extent of God's forgiveness for our own transgressions—"as ye shall sow, so shall ye reap." For this reason, Mother Teresa suggests, we are well advised to make a regular habit of righting the wrongs we have done to others.

"*People ask me what advice I have for a married couple struggling in their relationship. I always answer "Pray and forgive"; and to young people who come from violent homes, "Pray and forgive"; and to the single mother with no family support, "Pray and forgive".*"

MOTHER TERESA

EARTHLY REWARDS

WHEN WE DON'T FORGIVE, RESENTMENT AND anger can build up in body and mind, and the muscular and mental tension such negative emotions bring about may lead to physical, emotional, and even mental problems— insomnia, anxiety, hypertension, strokes and heart trouble, reduced immunity, headaches, loss of appetite or compensatory overeating have all been linked with such stress. The list of potential ailments could be longer. And these ailments aren't only debilitating for the sufferer; those around us have to deal with the consequences, too.

On the other hand, when we do manage to control our anger and resentment and find peace in forgiveness, stress-related problems can ease, and, as less adrenaline courses through the body, digestion and sleep patterns benefit, leading to increased ability to relax and enjoy life. We also save some of the precious energy previously wasted on futile emotions. Realizing how much time and effort spent in rage could have fueled more practical projects might be just the thing to prompt us to say "enough is enough." And inner peace only increases the peace worldwide: You can bet your bottom dollar that your family, friends, and colleagues will benefit enormously from living and working with a sunnier, destressed, more relaxed you.

FORGIVENESS AND HEALING

THE NEW TESTAMENT GOSPELS TELL OF THE beliefs surrounding sickness and health when Jesus began his ministry. Health was thought an example of God's will: Illness that could strike without reason was assumed to be a divine punishment for sins; a return to health was regarded as God's forgiveness and mercy. The fact that a sufferer might not be an obvious sinner was yet more proof that sickness was a divine mystery. This common-sense interpretation passed into religious law. So when Jesus was heard to advise the sick that their faith had made them whole

(Matthew 9:2–7) and their sins had been forgiven, accompanied by miraculous healing, it seemed Jesus had assumed a prerogative that belonged exclusively with God, which was blasphemous. Today, it may seem that science, not God, determines when a patient's health is restored, but to those of faith, God's role remains undiminished. God is within the surgeon's hands and the physician's art, and healing remains a divine gift.

"And, behold, they brought to him a man sick of the palsy, lying on a bed: and Jesus seeing their faith said unto the sick of the palsy; Son, be of good cheer; thy sins be forgiven thee.
And, behold, certain of the scribes said within themselves, This man blasphemeth."

THE GOSPEL OF ST. MATTHEW 9: 2–3

PARABLE

Jesus in the Temple

At the time of Jesus, though God's will was beyond question, there remained a human tendency to plead for divine sympathy when sick. It was commonplace for sufferers or their relatives to commission sacrifices from temple officials in the hope of winning God's mercy and forgiveness, and thereby the restoration of health. The commission of these offerings became a good source of income for temple officiates, since they acted as professional intermediaries with God. The use of a sacred place for this activity, with the associated stalls for money lending, and the selling of sacrificial offerings, greatly angered Jesus. He evicted these traders from the temple grounds, much to their annoyance. The anger of temple officiates fuelled a growing fire of jealous hatred for Jesus and his teaching.

Priests and traditionalists who heard Jesus's statements and witnessed the miraculous healings were enraged. If God alone might judge a person's sin and forgive his or her transgressions, and God alone could heal, the acts of mercy occurring around Jesus were sure-fire proof of His blasphemy, and must be the work of the devil. Fear and lack of understanding fed the jealousy and the mounting anger surrounding Jesus and his work. The growing popularity of this teacher who could heal the sick, and even, some said, raise the dead, made him a threat to the established religious and political order. He dared to see beyond the sin to the sinner, and knew the loving God forgives a true penitent.

THE GOSPEL OF ST. MATTHEW 21

"All the prophets testify about him that everyone who believes in him receives forgiveness of sins through his name."

ACTS 10:43

PART 2

Reasons for Forgiving

THOUGH LESS THAN THE CHRISTIAN ideal, one of the most persuasive reasons for forgiving others is that if the situation were reversed, we would hope to be granted forgiveness ourselves. At the very least, we ought to behave as we would have others behave. We are told in the Bible to love our neighbor as much as we love ourselves, so it is not enough to grudgingly mutter "sorry" if, deep inside, we are not. Truly granting forgiveness is a selfless act.

We forgo the urge to demand a confession or apology, as instinctive as that may be. When we recognize our own frailty in others's weakness, and spontaneously forgive them, we see God's love in action.

Granting or receiving forgiveness gives each of us the opportunity to make a fresh start, a chance to begin again and do better next time. It has nothing to do with finding justice, nor with forgetting any wrongs that have been done.

Through forgiveness we free ourselves from the cycle of bitterness and anger that builds up around wrongs done to us in the past, and as we liberate ourselves, so we free others from the burden of their guilt, too. The chain of action and reaction stops right there. Thus, forgiveness is one of the most powerful examples of love in action. It opens the door to personal freedom and renewed faith, and creates a means to heal damaged relationships day by day.

"The ability to forgive others ultimately comes from the humble recognition that we are all flawed and all human and if the roles were reversed we could have been the aggressor rather than the victim."

ARCHBISHOP DESMOND TUTU

WHO SUFFERS WHEN THERE IS NO FORGIVENESS?

WHEN WE DON'T FORGIVE, FRIENDS, FAMILY, AND colleagues can be adversely affected, too. Taking a chance on forgiveness has to be less damaging than holding onto pain or feelings of guilt, which only magnify the original offence.

What lack of forgiveness can bring

⟡ Pent up resentment and anger: over time, emotional fragility has harmful implications for health, and existing and future relationships may suffer.

❖ A reluctance to assume responsibility for emotional health: not resolving inner pain may lead to bad social decisions (by individuals, groups, and even nations).

❖ A craving for revenge: this hurts the avenger, as avenging actions become indistinguishable from those of the original wrongdoer. The victim changes places with the aggressor and becomes worthy of equal condemnation. The world's sum of aggression is increased by retaliation, not cancelled out by it.

❖ Living in the past at the expencse of the present, and future. Choosing misery when we might choose, and share, joy.

"The past is dead, forget it,
The future does not exist, don't worry,
Today is here, use it."

ANON

FORGIVENESS FOR A
HAPPIER FUTURE

YOU CAN MAKE AN INVESTMENT IN A HAPPIER
present by releasing the past; and change a
position of weakness into one of power
through an act of genuine forgiveness. In the
process of intending forgiveness you free
yourself from negative attachments to past
events. The deed was done—the past is
over—and if your inability to forgive keeps
the pain reactivated daily with each new rec-
ollection, you can find solace in forgiveness.
Remember that it is what you do today that
matters, and knowing that can bring a welcome sense of relief. Let the past be the past
at last and make room for the present.

FROM HEART TO HEART

IT IS THE HUMAN CONDITION TO MAKE MISTAKES. Forgiving does not condone a bad act, and punishment should be meted out according to the law. Forgiveness, however, is for the heart, not for the law. Whatever the transgression, it was the action that was wrongful, but it is from soul to soul that forgiveness is given. We humans grant forgiveness after judging the circumstances, perhaps after an apology, and only if the personal cost is not too great and the rewards are worthwhile. We judge others by our own standards of good and proper behavior. We determine preconditions before deciding whether to forgive or not; and yet we can never be possessed of all the facts when we make a judgment. God's forgiveness requires no preconditions and demands no prior apologies. It is given unconditionally.

Daily ways to ensure God's forgiveness

- ✤ Remember constantly that Jesus died for our sins.
- ✤ Be aware of your own failings and God's continued grace toward you.
- ✤ Never fail to extend sincere forgiveness to others.
- ✤ Do not forgive under coercion or to gain your own forgiveness.

The King and his Ungrateful Servant

Jesus shows how our behavior may be judged if we are not mindful of God's grace in the story of a servant forgiven his misdemeanors and released from debt by his compassionate master, a king. But the servant does not live in remembrance of this generosity, nor of the miserable fate he would have suffered without the intervention. Later, when his own servant similarly pleads for mercy, he lacks compassion. He forgets his debt of gratitude, and is made to suffer when the king finds out. The king and ungrateful servant are analogous to God and man. If we accept God's grace but fail to honor the source of our fortune and extend it to others, we are cast out.

THE GOSPEL OF ST. MATTHEW 18: 23–35

ARE YOU READY TO FORGIVE?
A Questionnaire

THESE FEW QUESTIONS HELP REVEAL YOUR expectations and general approach to life and other people. These expectations may dictate your ability to forgive, be forgiven, and to experience joy. There are no right or wrong answers, here; use a separate piece of paper to write down your thoughts to each question, then take some time to ponder the picture they build up. Consider how your answers reflect the way in which you think and behave, and muse on what you might like to change.

❖ If a good experience happens to you, do you automatically look for reasons why it will not last?

❖ Are you less comfortable with praise than with criticism?

❖ Do you feel you deserve to be happy?

❖ Do you fear that other people will dislike you if you enjoy good fortune; do you believe friendship depends on sharing miseries?

❖ Can material acquisitions or food compensate for unhappiness?

❖ How do you feel when you buy more things than you need or over-indulge?

✧ Do these activities blunt or mask a deeper craving or need for affection?

✧ In childhood did you feel loved and appreciated for yourself?

✧ Were you hurt and angry so often in the past that you are suspicious or afraid of happiness?

✧ Do you believe that suffering is a necessary part of life?

✧ Is happiness only to be expected in another life, never in this one?

✧ Do you expect to be happy at some future time? If so, what will have changed to make that possible?

⬧ Is happiness impossible now?

⬧ Are you afraid to forgive?

⬧ If you decide not to grant forgiveness, could anyone else do it on your behalf? How would this help you?

⬧ Would you feel disloyal, to yourself or others, if by forgiving a wrongdoer you were freed from bitterness?

⬧ Who would be pleased to see you happy, and how does that make you feel?

⬧ Who would be irritated if you were happy, and why?

⬧ Can you forgive someone today?

PART 3

How to Start Forgiving

I N THE LORD'S PRAYER WE LEARN that our trespasses (misdeeds) will be forgiven when we realize how we need God's forgiveness every bit as much as those who we now struggle to forgive. When we understand that we all sin at times, yet God continually forgives us, then, as Christians, we can do no less than forgive those whose behavior has let them, and us, down. Here are ways to start introducing those necessary, simple acts into daily life.

LITTLE DAILY FORGIVENESSES

THE SIMPLEST WAY TO START THE HABIT OF forgiving is to practice everyday in seemingly insignificant ways. In the morning, forgive the person whose slow driving seems sure to make you late for work: it may be God's way of protecting you from danger further ahead on the highway. In the office, forgive the harsh words from the colleague who knows no better: remember you have uttered worse words in your time. At lunchtime, forgive the storekeeper who shortchanges you, as you have done yourself on occasions by neglecting to hand back an erroneous banknote.

"Then came Peter to him, and said, Lord, how oft shall my brother sin against me, and I forgive him? Till seven times? Jesus saith unto him, I say not unto thee, Until seven times: but, Until seventy times seven."

THE GOSPEL OF ST. MATTHEW 18: 21–2

SMALL ACTS OF KINDNESS

FORGIVENESS IS EXTENDED TO US THROUGH God's mercy however often we stray from the path. Again and again we are forgiven every day and in every way by our Father. In return, we must forgive others every time we feel wronged. Though this demands time, will, and repeated effort, you can make every day a chance to be proud of yourself, even if only in small acts of generosity: Allow another person to go before you at the supermarket checkout, especially when you see someone who is frail or has only a few items. Give up a seat on public transport to a pregnant woman or someone with unwieldy luggage or small children. Offer to shop for a housebound neighbor. Befriend the student who joins the class mid-term and knows no one. Smile at your neighbor and exchange a few words when standing in line. Paying a little extra care and attention to others reaps rewards, and not just in heaven. It makes the world a happier and more generous place and spreads the kind of good feeling that encourages others to behave more thoughtfully, too.

"If we do not learn to live together as friends, we will die apart as fools."

MARTIN LUTHER KING, JR.

DO A GOOD DEED

DO YOU RECALL THE PRACTICE RANDOM ACTS OF Kindness and Senseless Beauty movement in the U.S.A.? Many people passing through tollgates on highways paid their own fee plus the toll for whoever followed next, though who that might be was quite unknown. This generous anarchy spread to become a popular movement leaving free tickets in other venues for unknown benefactors. People enjoyed how a small act of generosity made them feel, and it pleased those who benefited from the free pass. The custom spread, creating widespread happiness for as long as it

lasted. How much more worthwhile than taking every petty opportunity to defraud (an act
that leaves the cheater more diminished than
the cheated). If you look for ways to be kind,
the reward that flows back to you in reciprocal good feeling far outweighs the minimal
effort. You surround yourself with positive
energy, which invites yet more positivity.

*"The practice of forgiveness is our most
important contribution to the healing of
the world."*
MARIANNE WILLIAMSON

NIGHTLY REMEMBRANCE

FEW OF US CAN FORGIVE THOSE WHO HURT US AS readily as Christ did in His agony. Although we know as Christians we ought to forgive those who have acted dishonorably toward us; in honesty, it's hard. But an inability to forgive just adds an additional daily burden of guilt and shame, anger and despair to the original sense of injury. Try each night before sleep to work on reducing this heavy load, by giving up a little to God.

"One of the secrets of a long and fruitful life is to forgive everybody everything every night before you go to bed."

ANN LANDERS

"Every night before you go to bed you must make an examination of conscience (because you don't know if you will be alive in the morning!) Whatever is troubling you, or whatever wrong you may have done, you need to repair it. Remember that God is merciful, He is the merciful father to us all. We are His children and he will forgive and forget if we remember to do so."

FROM *THE BOOK OF PEACE* BY MOTHER TERESA

STOP SNAPPING

WHEN YOU ARE FEELING IRRITATED BY SOME-
one's words or deeds, stop and consider who
is really suffering. Why, it's you, of course!
Petty aggravations do nothing for your state of
wellbeing nor your good relationships with
other people. You can choose whether you
treat each moment of potential rage as an
opportunity to practice Christian forgiveness
and compassion, or simply to throw another
log on the fire of your anger.

KEEPING TO THE PATH

CHRISTIANITY HAS A LONG TRADITION OF pilgrimage on foot—of walking as a form of self-examination, as a way of seeking forgiveness, and as a physical means of emptying body and mind, ready to be filled with remembrance of God's love. Pilgrims traditionally follow a track walked for centuries to a sacred site, such as the Cathedral in Santiago de Compostela in northern Spain. But you might equally take a contemplative stroll at lunchtime to a favourite chapel or natural wonder. Why not make a daily walk the starting point for your journey within?

PARABLE

The Man Who Built His House on Rock

"…whosoever believeth in Him shall receive forgiveness of sins."

ACTS 10:43

If we know we are commanded to remember and be grateful for God's mercy toward us yet do not live our lives in that remembrance, we are like the man who builds his house on a foundation of sand. However fancy and ornate the property, once bad weather strikes, it will collapse. The wise man, Jesus says, is the one who builds a house on firm foundations. This man builds a structure that can withstand the onslaught of every type of weather. Think of daily remembrance of God's will and generosity toward us as like building a house on rock. When we are tested by hard times, the structure (firm knowledge of God's love and mercy) is in place to support and protect us. When we need forgiveness, it will be there, too.

THE GOSPEL OF ST. MATTHEW 7: 26–27

TEACHING CHILDREN THE ART
OF FORGIVENESS

CHILDREN ARE A POWERFUL REASON FOR learning to forgive. What we say and do affects the attitudes of the young people who look to us for guidance, and, like it or not, they learn from our example. If the experiences of the next generation are to be positive, we must learn to deal with our sources of pain and, through forgiveness, offer them an affirmative example. You can start while your children are still surprisingly young, using some of the practical strategies set out on pages 58–59. How much easier it is to forgive and be forgiven as an adult when you've been doing so every day since infancy.

"Forgiveness is the answer to the child's dream of a miracle by which what is broken is made whole again, what is soiled is again made clean."

DAG HAMMARSKJÖLD

FIRST STEPS

⬧ Lead by example. Show that you forgive wrongdoers despite the harm they have done you; this offers young people a tangible way to handle painful situations constructively rather than become the victim of them.

⬧ Whatever wrong you have experienced, let it end with you. Do not make hatred and bitterness your legacy to the next generation. You have a choice, so make sure you are seen to use it.

❖ Encourage children to spend some quiet
time each day thinking about the people
they love, and feeling the warmth of this
connection. This very simple act can
boost understanding and kindness.

❖ Before bed while children are still young,
introduce a time to say sorry for the little
misdeeds of the day, for arguing with a
sibling, for example, or being unkind to a
school friend.

"Modern man listens more readily
To witnesses than to teachers,
And if he listens to teachers
It is because they are witnesses."

POPE PAUL VI

BUT I'M A LAPSED CHRISTIAN...

JESUS EXPLAINS THE QUALITY OF GOD'S FOR-giveness in parables (teaching stories) that remind us it is never too late to return to the path. He uses the stories of a father who thought he had lost his son, and of a shepherd who thought he had lost a sheep, to reassure us that there will always be a welcome waiting for the penitent. Both stories illustrate how genuine penitence will be rewarded and tell how a sinner may always return to the pro-tection of the church (his Father) if she or he repents. Both stories are set out and analyzed on the pages that follow.

The Prodigal Son

"And he said, A certain man had two sons:

And the younger of them said to his father, Father, give me the portion of goods that falleth to me. And he divided unto them his living.

And not many days after the younger son gathered all together, and took his journey into a far country, and there wasted his substance with riotous living.

And when he had spent all, there arose a mighty famine in that land; and he began to be in want.

And he went and joined himself to a citizen of that country; and he sent him into his fields to feed swine.

And he would fain have filled his belly with the husks that the swine did eat: and no man gave unto him.

And when he came to himself, he said,

How many hired servants of my father's have bread enough and to spare, and I perish with hunger!

I will arise and go to my father, and will say unto him, Father, I have sinned against heaven, and before thee,

And I am no more worthy to be called thy son; make me as one of thy hired servants.

And he arose, and came to his father. But when he was yet a great way off, his father saw him, and had compassion, and ran, and fell on his neck, and kissed him.

And the son said unto him, father, I have sinned against heaven, and in thy sight, and am no more worthy to be called thy son.

The father said to his servants, Bring forth the best robe, and put it on him; put a ring on his hand, and shoes on his feet:

And bring hither the fatted calf, and kill

it; and let us eat, and be merry:

For this my son was dead, and is alive again; he was lost, and is found. And they began to be merry.

Now his elder son was in the field: and as he came and drew nigh to the house, he heard musick and dancing.

And he called one of the servants, and asked what these things meant.

And he said unto him, Thy brother is come; and thy father hath killed the fatted calf, because he hath received him safe and sound.

And he was angry, and would not go in: therefore came his father out, and intreated him.

And he answering said to his father, Lo, these many years do I serve thee, neither transgressed I at any time thy command-

ment: and yet thou never gavest me a kid, that I might make merry with my friends:

But as soon as this thy son was come, which hath devoured thy living with harlots, thou hast killed for him the fatted calf.

And he said unto him, Son, thou art ever with me, and all that I have is thine.

It was meet that we should make merry, and be glad: for this thy brother was dead, and is alive again; and was lost, and is found."

THE GOSPEL OF ST. LUKE 15:11–32

ANALYZING THE STORY

THE FATHER FORGIVES HIS RECKLESSLY IMMORAL and extravagant (prodigal) son after he confesses, repents, and changes his ways. The wayward son regains his place in the family on an equal footing with a brother who had not strayed and wasted his share of his inheritance. This seems unfair to the sensible brother: Had he acted similarly foolhardily, then sincerely regretted it and confessed, his father would have forgiven him, too, but he is so hurt at what seems unjust treatment that he cannot consider this possibility. He prefers bitter complaint and refuses to celebrate the wastrel's return. The dutiful son finds it impossible to forgive his brother, though their father—the only person actually wronged—joyously does so. How many of us would find it similarly hard to forgive, much less celebrate, when one who has wronged us says "sorry" and expects the slate to be wiped clean? We also might feel punishment is more appropriate than celebration. The story of the prodigal son teaches how heartfelt penitence and confession will lead to our reinstatement in God's grace, if we need enough, and want little enough. The boy was willing to become a servant (wanting little), and was starving and full of regret (feeling in great need). The compassionate father of the story is the counterpart of God. Our heavenly Father would welcome us, if we returned to Him, having realized the error of our ways.

"Blessed is he whose transgression is forgiven, whose sin is covered."

PSALMS 32:1

The Lost Sheep

"Now the tax collectors and 'sinners' were all gathering around to hear him [Jesus].

But the Pharisees and the teachers of the law muttered. 'This man welcomes sinners and eats with them.'

Then Jesus told them this parable: 'Suppose one of you has a hundred sheep and loses one of them. Does he not leave the ninety-nine in the open country and go after the lost sheep until he finds it?

And when he finds it, he joyfully puts it on his shoulders and calls his friends and neighbors together and says, "Rejoice with me; I have found my lost sheep."

I tell you that in the same way there will be more rejoicing in heaven over one sinner who repents than over ninety-nine righteous persons who do not need to repent.'"

THE GOSPEL OF ST. LUKE 15: 1–7

ANALYZING THE STORY

JESUS TELLS THIS TALE TO MAKE THE SAME point. This time a shepherd welcomes the return of one sheep he had lost, though he still has a flock of ninety-nine others that did not leave him. We, too, shall be welcomed back to a place of safety and protection when we repent of our wrongdoing and determine to change our ways. The love and forgiveness we receive from God (here, the shepherd) is beyond our limited ideas of what is fair. The forgivable (the rest of the flock), are safe and need no immediate attention. It is the "unforgivable" lost sheep that needs our love.

So it is when we can find it in our hearts to be penitent for our own sins, to genuinely regret the past, and seek to make amends. No one can unsay a cross word already spoken. No act can be undone. We can only sincerely repent and be willing to accept whatever we have coming, as the prodigal son was willing to be reduced to servitude in exchange for his father's food and shelter. Heart to heart, God's love is beyond measure when we are sincere. It is we who turn our face from Him. His face ever remains turned toward us, like the prodigal son's father, scanning the horizon, hoping to see his son's return.

PRAYERS, POEMS,

and

THOUGHTS

of

FORGIVENESS

"Our Father which art in heaven,
Hallowed be thy name.
Thy kingdom come.
Thy will be done in earth,
as it is in heaven.
Give us this day our daily bread.
And forgive us our debts,
as we forgive our debtors.
And lead us not into temptation,
but deliver us from evil:
For thine is the kingdom, and the power,
and the glory, for ever. Amen."

THE LORD'S PRAYER
THE GOSPEL OF ST. MATTHEW 6:9–13

"My Lord, I love You. My God, I am sorry. My God, I believe in You. My God, I trust You. Help us to love one another as You love us."

MOTHER TERESA

"Lord, make me an instrument of Your peace, ✧ *Where there is hatred let me sow love;* ✧ *Where there is injury, pardon:* ✧ *Where there is doubt, faith;* ✧ *Where there is despair, hope;* ✧ *Where there is darkness, light, and* ✧ *Where there is sadness, joy.* ✧ *O divine master,* ✧

Grant that I may not so much ❖ *Seek to be consoled as to console;* ❖ *To be understood as to understand;* ❖ *To be loved as to love;* ❖ *For it is in giving that we receive;* ❖ *It is in pardoning that we are pardoned, and* ❖ *In dying that we are born to eternal life."*

ST. FRANCIS OF ASSISI

"He died, declaring God's forgiveness. He rose on the third day, transforming death. He ascended into heaven that he might be everywhere on earth. He sent the Holy Spirit as the seal of his intention. He sets before us bread and wine, and invites us to his table. This is the place where we are made well again."

FROM THE IONA COMMUNITY
COMMUNION LITURGY

"Forgive me, Lord, for Thy dear Son,
The ill that I this day have done;
That with the World, myself and Thee,
I, ere I sleep, at peace may be."

THOMAS KEN, BISHOP OF BATH

"Create in me a clean heart, O God;
and renew a right spirit within me.
Cast me not away from thy presence;
and take not thy holy spirit from me.
Restore unto me the joy of thy salvation;
and uphold me with thy free spirit.
Then will I teach transgressors thy ways;
and sinners shall be converted unto thee."

PSALM 51: 10–13

*"O pitying One,
Thy pity is from the foundation of the
world, and Thy
Redemption
Begins already in Eternity."*

WILLIAM BLAKE

PART 4

Forgiving Yourself

GIVE YOURSELF THE GIFT OF FORGIVE-ness. Give up the vain hope that by holding on to a hurt you somehow might make the past better. This moment is all you have. You cannot change past moments. When you let them go and happiness returns, you will be in a much more secure and contented frame of mind from which to find a way to forgive those who hurt you. It's your choice to allow a different attitude to develop. Happiness is with you.

LETTING IT GO

SEEK FORGIVENESS FOR YOUR OWN MISGUIDED acts and it helps you find a way to forgive others for theirs. Maybe you need to forgive yourself for something only you know about. So long as you hold onto feelings of guilt, shame, or anger you burden yourself to no one's benefit. Make restitution if you can, and, whatever the situation, be as compassionate with yourself as you would be with a friend. You probably view your misdemeanor more harshly than anyone else would—even the person you feel you wronged. We set higher standards for ourselves than we would for others. How would you counsel a friend who regretted the act for which you need to forgive yourself? Can you imagine Jesus would berate you or fail to extend His compassion? Why decide you deserve a harsher judgment than He would give?

"Only the brave know how to forgive.
A coward never forgave; it is not in
his nature."

LAURENCE STERNE

"But we sin whenever we are less than we could be, when we miss the mark of our potential to be fully loving and caring human beings. These smaller sins also need *forgiveness, as of course do the larger violations of one another's humanity and holiness, but asking for forgiveness... requires humility, as does granting forgiveness."*

ARCHBISHOP DESMOND TUTU

FESSIN' UP

IT'S GOOD IF YOU HAVE THE NEED TO FEEL FOR-
given. As Christians, we always have a chance
to do better than we did, but we must first
admit errors to God and ourselves, if to no
one else. Christian forgiveness is conditional
upon sincere repentance. God may forgive
all, but first we must repent of our past
actions and forgive those who acted against
us. Then we can start to deal with the suffering we feel or have created for others.
Admitting the error of our ways is the first
step to peace.

*"If God were not willing to forgive sin,
Heaven would be empty."*

GERMAN PROVERB

"He who forgives ends a quarrel."

AFRICAN PROVERB

I'M NOT THAT BAD, ACTUALLY

ARE YOU FAULTLESS AT ALL TIMES? THE SIN-FREE have no need of redemption. Think about it again. Have you never needed forgiveness? The Christian knows forgiveness beyond measure is available to all who repent.

"If we say that we have no sin, we deceive ourselves and the truth is not in us. If we confess our sins, he is faithful and just to forgive us our sins, and to cleanse us from all unrighteousness. If we say that we have not sinned, we make him a liar, and his word is not in us."

1 JOHN 1: 8–10

"Denial is a human capacity too, and many of us deny wrongdoing, failing to acknowledge responsibility. We may insist that what we did was right after all, or argue that it was partially or fully excusable. ... All these possibilities underline the basic fact that as human beings and moral agents, we are capable of fresh starts and the kind of fundamental change that is moral transformation."

TRUDY GOVIER

"One of the ways the human animal has learned to deal with the pain of the past is by burying it behind a fog of denial. It is as though we know instinctively that if we look too closely at the thing that was done to us it will completely paralyze us, so we

hide it from ourselves like a mad relative in the back room of the basement. But its presence down there leaches into our lives anyway, affecting our relationships and our general conduct in ways we ourselves probably never fully comprehend."

RICHARD HOLLOWAY

RECOGNIZING SIN

IF WE ARE HONEST, WE ALL KNOW WE ARE capable of failing each other, given the right day and the right trigger. Whatever the magnitude of our lapses from grace, the same inclination lies behind each one. Who can say that given the same provocation as someone we find difficult to forgive we could not have felt motivated to behave the same way? If we can separate a person from their deeds, forgiveness becomes a little easier. We can choose to forgive those who fail us, just as we trust our failures toward others will also be forgiven.

"For if ye forgive men their trespasses, your heavenly father will also forgive you."

THE GOSPEL OF ST. MATTHEW 6:14

TAKING RESPONSIBILITY

WE MUST ALL TAKE PERSONAL RESPONSIBILITY for our actions. Christians do not cause harm to others, even when to exact personal revenge for some slight might be most inviting. To do so would enmesh us even deeper in pain, since we would then have to bear the additional burden of having acted no better than the original sinner, who no doubt had good reasons too. Scores are not leveled by retaliation. They are doubled. There are positive ways to live with pain when to forgive is still out of the question. There are also ways to limit the debilitating effects of living with rage. We will take a look at some of these positive practices in chapter seven (pages 237–98) as coping strategies rather than as an acceptance of defeat.

"He who cannot forgive breaks the bridge over which he himself must pass."

GEORGE HERBERT

DECIDING TO CHANGE

IF YOU CAUSED HURT TO ANOTHER FOR WHICH you seek forgiveness, take some positive steps to ensure that you would not act in the same way again, whatever the provocation might be. Learn to control yourself by following some of the practical strategies and action plans set out in chapter seven (pages 237–98). Forgiveness without an intent to change is nothing more than hollow rhetoric. It might be helpful to take some counseling, if it is within your means and you think it may help you. This makes another positive step toward the change you have decided to make. It is always important to commit through action, not just in words or good intentions. Change may not be easy or immediate—in many cases it might be the most demanding task you have ever set yourself—but forgiveness is worth working at, and so are you.

"When a deep injury is done us, we never recover until we forgive."

ALAN PATON

LOOKING WITHIN

IT IS NO GOOD FOR SOMEONE TO TELL YOU TO forgive the architect of your pain when you cannot even forgive yourself. When you feel anger and hatred for someone, it is often a projection of the anger and hatred you have for yourself. You find faults in others that you know you exhibit yourself, and are thus irritated by having them brought to your notice. When you have compassion for your own failings, you will find yourself more tolerant of the failings of others. So it is with forgiveness. That which you cannot forgive in another you cannot forgive in yourself.

Until we recognize that all of us share the potential for wrongdoing and also share a common hope for redemption through sincere regret and the desire to act better in future, we cannot reclaim a future free from the emotional tatters of the past. Nor can we expect to be forgiven for our own lapses since we have ruled out forgiveness to others. The Bible is clear on this point.

"This is my commandment, that ye love one another as I have loved you."

THE GOSPEL OF ST. JOHN 15:12

"Dear Lord and Father of mankind.
Forgive our foolish ways
Reclothe us in our rightful mind
In purer lives thy service find
In deeper reverence praise."

J.G. WHITTIER

SELF-EXAM

THE FIRST STEP TO FORGIVENESS, WHEN WE ARE ready and willing to take it, is to examine the truth of our feelings. What cannot be contemplated cannot be forgiven, and what cannot be forgiven cannot be overcome, though it may be accommodated, so we must begin by honestly acknowledging what has happened and offering it up to God. This may sound foolish. Of course you know what happened, and God certainly does. However, there is a world of difference between knowing the historical facts, and consciously admitting them to yourself and to God. Start by owning up to what you felt then and what you feel now, and try to explain why you reacted so, without making excuses for your actions (or lack of action). What matters most is expressing truthfully the feelings that these actions stirred within you.

"Forgiveness means that you do not hold others responsible for your experiences."

GARY ZUKAV

BRINGING DOWN THE BARRIERS

TO RELEARN NEW WAYS WE MUST FIRST COME TO an understanding that the old ways of being do not serve us well. If the payoff for habitual behavior patterns ceases to benefit us, we may decide to reform, but if the fear of dropping our protective wall of unfeeling is too great, we may never change. Does this mean we should never be forgiven either? Begin by considering the barriers you yourself have to granting forgiveness, and think about whether they are justified. Have you ever reacted from a place of pain without consideration for another person, for instance? Jesus, perhaps recalling his experiences in Joseph's carpentry shop, advises us to attend to the speck of dust in our own eye before being too quick to notice the plank in another person's. It is easy to spot a fault in another person and overlook the fact that we share the same tendency.

"And why beholdest thou the mote that is in thy brother's eye, but considerest not the beam that is in thine own eye? Or how wilt thou say to thy brother, Let me pull out the mote out of thine eye; and, behold, a beam is in thine own eye? Thou hypocrite, first cast out the beam out of thine own eye; and then shalt thou see clearly to cast out the mote out of thy brother's eye."

THE GOSPEL OF ST. MATTHEW 7: 3–5

LOVING YOURSELF

FORGIVING ONESELF AS ONE WOULD FORGIVE others can be the hardest task of all. When you are able to forgive, you are able to embrace the love and wholeness that was always within you instead of the damaged, personal view that seemed to splinter it. After forgiving yourself, you are more likely to be willing to risk trust and hope again, instead of living with fear and despair. In the process you will lift the pain you have carried. You are as worthy and as deserving of love and happiness as any other being. You are so much more than your hurts, fears, mistakes, and self-doubt. You are whole and complete as you are, and do not need to repay debts created by "unfair" events. Bad things happen to us all; they do not denote a bad person or suggest you deserve unhappiness more than anyone else. They are what shape you, for good or ill.

"We pardon to the extent that we love."
LA ROUCHEFOUCHAULD

"God will forgive me; it is His trade."

HEINRICH HEINE

SO WHAT'S STOPPING YOU?

SAD TO SAY, BUT UNTIL YOU CAN FORGIVE yourself, you are unlikely to be able to forgive anyone else; even the gospels tell us this. If you feel you are the victim of a misdeed, you may ask what forgiveness you could possibly need. Surely you have no reason to seek forgiveness from anyone when you were the victim of the situation, not its agent? The questions on the following pages might start you thinking and help you begin to unravel the twists of time.

Questions to Ponder

❖ Do you feel partly responsible for an event, or fear you might have done more to prevent what happened?

❖ How about the times you betrayed your higher aspirations and behaved badly, then criticized yourself because of your actions?

❖ Have you forgiven yourself for times when you acted out of fear, were judgmental, or unkind? Why do you imagine you acted that way?

❖ Have you forgiven yourself for needing love so much that you went to extreme lengths to feel loved?

❖ Do you feel you acted in some way that encouraged a bad experience; maybe you should have said something sooner, or taken a different route; should have listened to your intuition, or what others tried to warn you of? Do you feel responsible, or partially responsible, for a failure to act? Are these such awful crimes?

STOP SPREADING THE HURT

HAVE YOU EVER LOST YOUR TEMPER WITH AN innocent person because you were still annoyed at a slight or hurt someone caused you earlier? Have you been on the receiving end of an outburst totally out of proportion to the current situation? When we fail to deal with our pain constructively, we risk spreading it around in such ways. Jesus teaches us to live life in daily remembrance of God and awareness of how much we owe Him. If we live this way and know how many times we have been forgiven, we may find it a little easier to forgive ourselves and then to forgive others.

"Strive to be patient; bear with the faults and frailties of others, for you, too, have many faults which others have to bear…"

THOMAS À KEMPIS

LIGHTEN UP

GET IN THE HABIT OF FORGIVING YOURSELF AND, suddenly, forgiving other people becomes that much easier. How we feel about ourselves affects the ways in which we relate to and interact with others. It's hard to extend or receive any emotional quality we are incapable of feeling or understanding ourselves. Likewise, other people take their cues from us, and so if we feel and act ashamed, those around us feel uncomfortable, which makes us think our poor self esteem was justified. Without wishing to make light of some of the reasons for suffering, most of us, if we can make light of our own troubles with a shrug of exasperation and a ready smile, will find willing helpers in the struggle to forgive and a smile in return. If we can be forgiving of others' wrongdoing, we are so much more likely to be able to accept forgiveness when it is offered for our own sins.

"For a long time it had seemed to me that life was about to begin—real life. But there was always some obstacle in the way, something to be got through first, some unfinished business, time still to be served, a debt to be paid. Then life would begin. At last it dawned on me that these obstacles were my life."

FR. ALFRED D'SOUZA

GETTING OVER BLAME

IT CAN SOMETIMES BE EASIER TO BLAME ourselves than those really responsible. It can also be easier to blame others than accept that random crimes and tragedies happen all the time. There need be no pre-motivation, justification, or sense to what happened. All that is required is to be unlucky enough to be at the wrong place at the wrong time, by pure chance. Had it not been you or your loved one it would have been someone else. Would that have been any more just?

"Asking for forgiveness requires that we take responsibility for our part in the rupture that has occurred in the relationship. We can always make excuses for ourselves and find justifications for our actions, however contorted, but we know that these keep us locked in the prison of blame and shame."

ARCHBISHOP DESMOND TUTU

MOVING ON

MOST OF US HAVE A TENDENCY TO RELIVE THE past in our imagination, whether we found it good or ill, each time recreating a slightly different truth regardless of what actually happened. We base our expectations of the future on these reinvented memories, and daydream of a future that will never be, since we can never include all the unforeseen influences that subtly, or not so subtly, alter our best laid plans. We all have biased or incomplete memories, even of events we witnessed. It's been suggested, humorously, that we remember the future and imagine the past, because of this tendency, when all we truly have is now. The effort involved in maintaining anger and hatred or self-loathing does nothing to change the truth of what happened. It is over. Holding onto the pain, embarrassment, or anger forces us to revisit the past constantly, and this infects the present, time and time again. We lose hope and the willingness to trust and can become infected with a pervasive cynicism that belittles every good thing. However, merely to be seen to forgive is not the same as genuine forgiving from the heart. Only the latter, with penitence and faith, and a determination to behave differently in future, can reconcile and transform lives.

"To forgive is to set a prisoner free and discover that the prisoner was you."

LEWIS SMEDES

ACCEPTING APOLOGIES

HOW ARE YOU AT FORGIVING WHEN APOLOGIZED to? Do you prefer to hold onto your anger and resentment? If so try thinking this way: The offender damaged you once, but you continue to damage yourself day in, day out, for the rest of your life, while the offender is free to move on. If you can find it in your heart to forgive, you can end this intolerable situation in which you suffer as much, if not more, than the subject of your anger. Choose to accept an apology and you are free to move into a brighter future.

DOUBLE STANDARDS

ARE YOU AS CRITICAL OF YOURSELF AS YOU ARE of others? Many people who aspire to a life of integrity and seem to be good Christians at home and in the community apply a double standard when it comes to business, telling themselves that unethical behavior is just smart trading. Society is to blame, we might retort, but what is a society but a collection of individuals? When is our unethical behavior no longer acceptable? When we are caught? Healing can only begin with honesty.

"...By being aimed at someone and not something, forgiveness becomes an act of love."

FROM *HANNAH ARENDT* BY JULIA KRISTEVA

"*Therefore all things whatsoever ye would that men should do to you, do ye even so to them...*"

MATTHEW 7:12

PRETENDING TO FORGIVE

THE DECISION TO FORGIVE HAS TO BE GENUINE and heartfelt, as the Bible makes clear, so let no one tell you must forgive if you feel you cannot. To pretend forgiveness because it is expected adds insult to injury. No one else knows how it is to walk in your shoes but, sadly, so long as you remain unable to forgive, you will be unable to free yourself from your past, and all aspects of the future will be negatively affected.

BUYING FORGIVENESS?

CHRISTIANS CANNOT BARTER WITH GOD AS A means to obtain His forgiveness. We cannot buy forgiveness by pretending that we have forgiven others or by doing good deeds with the thought of reward. To be forgiven, we must first sincerely feel forgiveness for those who upset us, and remember the many ways in which we, too, have hurt others. Our lapses may be lesser or greater than those we have suffered, but the difference is merely a product of individual circumstance, for the capacity to sin is a universal aspect of the human condition. We should forgive others because we know our situation and that of the wrongdoer might easily have been reversed, if it were not for God's grace and our different backgrounds, and we know how many times we have been forgiven for our misdemeanors. In happier times we sense God's embrace, and know we are loved and forgiven. We may even laugh at the human weaknesses we see in others because we know we share them. When others' actions cause us to suffer, it may not be so easy to remember the weaknesses we share.

THE WAY OUT

EACH TIME WE ARE CONFRONTED WITH AN ethical choice but act other than as Christ would have, we add another weight to the secret shame we bear, and deny ourselves the right to God's forgiveness. We may be the only one who knows what we did—apart from God—but we know, and the effort of trying to kid ourselves it doesn't matter, or to forget it, becomes a burden. God's mercy is available whatever our shameful past, if we freely repent and regret our wrongdoing, intend to do better in the future, and beg for forgiveness and mercy. If we do not intend to mend our ways and have no regret for our shameful acts, God will not forgive us. On this point the gospels are clear. First we repent, then we may be forgiven, but our repentance must be freely offered and sincere.

"And so John came, baptizing in the desert region and preaching a baptism of repentance for the forgiveness of sins."

THE GOSPEL OF ST. MARK 1:4,
REFERRING TO JOHN THE BAPTIST

DOES FORGIVENESS HAVE TO
BE RECIPROCAL?

WHAT IF WE WANT TO FORGIVE TO EASE OUR emotional burden after a traumatic event, but the forgiven person perceives no need for forgiveness, either because he does not care, or cannot see his actions as wrong? Forgiving, in such cases, may make us feel better, but cannot lead to a change in the offender. It might even make matters worse. To be effective, forgiveness must be reciprocal, greeted by an acceptance of wrongdoing and a desire for change. But what happens when no bridge of understanding or love can be built with a perpetrator; does the effectiveness of being forgiven become questionable? Christ led the way by forgiving his persecutors on the cross. We do not have to find the unacceptable acceptable when we grant forgiveness. That could never be sincere, but if we consider how many times and in how many ways God has forgiven us, it becomes easier to forgive those persons who have hurt or offended us without denying the evil of their actions.

"For if ye forgive men their trespasses, your heavenly Father will also forgive you: but if ye forgive not men their trespasses, neither will your Father forgive your trespasses."

THE GOSPEL OF ST. MATTHEW 6: 9–23

CHRIST'S FORGIVENESS
ON THE CROSS

ARE WE TO FORGIVE ONLY WHEN FORGIVENESS is sought? Christ gave us the answer when he forgave his tormentors from the cross: he forgave them because "they know not what they do." They were innocent of evil intent and so could not be expected to repent. Slaying the Son of God was not on the agenda of the Roman soldiers carrying out their quota of crucifixions for the day. (Crucifixion was a commonplace punishment at the time.) God compassionately forgives the person who in all innocence commits an evil act, but this does not imply He condones an evil deed in

any way. The offender whose twisted per-
spective sees no wrong in his actions cannot
be said to have evil intent.

MAKING A NEW START

NO SIN IS TOO GREAT FOR GOD'S MERCY AND forgiveness. Since perfection is not an option this side of heaven, there is no need to punish yourself, or others, continually for past lapses and errors of judgment. Do not take on that impossible burden in addition to tackling feelings of rage or regret, and do not expect perfection of others; you will only be disappointed. Even the Christian saints had their flaws. Saint Augustine, who was no stranger to worldly desires, tells us in his Confessions, "Give me chastity Lord ... and continence ... but not today." There spoke a man who was aware of his frailties. He knew he had strong appetites and that any pretence to behave otherwise would be less than heartfelt.

"Without being forgiven, released from the consequences of what we have done, our capacity to act would, as it were, be confined to one single deed from which we could never recover; we would remain the victim of its consequences forever..."

RICHARD HOLLOWAY

"Forgiveness gives us the capacity to make a new start. That is the power, the rationale, of confession and forgiveness. it is to say, 'I have fallen but I am not going to remain there. Please forgive me.' And forgiveness is the grace by which you enable the other person to get up, and get up *with dignity, to begin anew. Not to forgive leads to bitterness and hatred, which, just like self-hatred and self-contempt, gnaw away at the vitals of one's being. Whether hatred is projected out or projected in, it is always corrosive of the human spirit."*

ARCHBISHOP DESMOND TUTU

HELP IN THE FIRST INSTANCE

WE ARE NOT ABANDONED TO THE WHIM OF OUR assailants. We have only to ask to receive His help. He is a loving and ever-present Father. We are told in the Gospel according to St. Matthew that we have only to ask and we shall receive, to seek and we shall find, to knock and the door will be opened to us. God is waiting for us to initiate an intimate relationship with Him.

"Ask, and it shall be given you; seek, and
ye shall find; knock, and it shall be
opened unto you.
For every one that asketh receiveth; and
he that seeketh findeth; and to him that
knocketh it shall be opened.
Or what man is there of you, whom if his
son ask bread, will he give him a stone?
Or if he ask a fish,
will he give him a serpent?
If ye then, being evil, know how to give
good gifts unto your children, how much
more shall your Father which is in heaven
give good things to them that ask him?
Therefore all things whatsoever ye would
that men should do to you, do ye even so
to them: for this is the law and
the prophets."

THE GOSPEL OF ST. MATTHEW 7: 7–12

WHERE TO ASK FOR FORGIVENESS

CAN YOU ASK FORGIVENESS FROM THE PERSON you wronged? Before you do so, carefully consider the implications of your desire for absolution. If you suspect the truth of your confession would cause someone pain, take it to professionals instead; to a counselor or priest who will hear whatever you have to say in strict confidence and be equipped to release you from your burden of guilt. If you cannot bear to tell anyone, give your pain to God. His shoulders are broad enough to bear it and He will absolve you.

"What power has love but forgiveness?"

WILLIAM CARLOS WILLIAMS

STILL NEED SOME TIME?

PERHAPS IT IS TOO SOON TO THINK OF FORGIVE-
ness for yourself or for someone else. Give
yourself as much time as you need—and then
some, if necessary. The older the wound, the
more time you might need to start rethinking
your perception of it. Mull over exactly what
happened and the circumstances surrounding the event; think about what might have
rolled out differently, and what would always
have been beyond your control. Until you can
accept the truth of what happened and why it
took place, you cannot begin to forgive and
move on with your life. When and if you do so

is for you to decide. We do not fail when the honest response is, "I cannot." There are implications for the way in which we proceed once we know this of ourselves, but that we have the absolute right to express it should not be in doubt.

> *"Almost all our faults are more pardonable than the methods we think up to hide them."*
>
> ANON

PRAYERS

and

POEMS

of

FORGIVENESS

"Lord Jesus Christ,
Son of God,
Have mercy on me,
a sinner"

THE JESUS PRAYER

"Oh my Jesus, forgive us our sins, save us from the fires of hell and lead all souls to heaven, especially those in most need of your mercy. Amen."

THE FATIMA PRAYER, REPEATED AT THE
END OF EACH DECADE (GROUP OF TEN) BEADS
OF THE CATHOLIC ROSARY

I was angry with my friend:
I told my wrath, my wrath did end.
I was angry with my foe;
I told it not, my wrath did grow.

And I water'd it in fears,
Night & morning with my tears;
And I sunned it with my smiles
And with soft deceitful wiles.

And it grew both day and night,
Till it bore an apple bright;
And my foe beheld it shine,
And he knew that it was mine,

And into my garden stole
When the night had veil'd the pole:
In the morning glad I see
My foe outstretch'd beneath the tree ."

A "POISON TREE" BY WILLIAM BLAKE

"Wilt thou forgive that sinne where I begunne, ❖ Which is my sin, though it were done before? ❖ Wilt thou forgive those sinnes, through which I runne, ❖ And do run still: though still I do deplore? ❖ When thou hast done, thou hast not done, ❖ For, I have more. ❖ Wilt *thou forgive that sinne by which I have wonne* ❖ *Others to sinne? And, made my sinne their doore?* ❖ *Wilt though forgive that sinne which I did shunne* ❖ *A yeare, or two: but wallowed in, a score?* ❖ *When thou hast done, thou hast not done,* ❖ *For I have more."*

FROM 'TO GOD THE FATHER' BY JOHN DONNE

PART 5

Forgiving Others

I N THE SERMON ON THE MOUNT, JESUS teaches us to love unconditionally; not just when we are loved, or because the person is well known and liked by us. Anyone can do that, he says. If we want to be the Children of God, we should love and acknowledge others, as God does— even when it is difficult and challenging. No 'ifs' and 'buts', but unconditionally, just as God treats you. Here we offer ways to explore this important spiritual practice.

ESTABLISHING EMPATHY

THE CHRISTIAN WAY IS TO LOVE OUR ENEMIES AS well as our friends and neighbors (as we are urged in the Gospel of St.Matthew 7:1–6), for we will be judged by the same measure we use to judge others. Before we can find it in our hearts to forgive, many of us may need to consider how the offender was feeling when the sinful act was committed, as painful as that act of sympathy might be to contemplate. This exploration is not intended to bring about a lessening of the many wrongs you have suffered; with empathy may come the grounds for sincere forgiveness. Jesus set us an example of unconditional forgiveness that is inspirational, but we may need more conditional acts of understanding and empathy before we, too, can learn to forgive, for we are only human.

"Be kind and compassionate to one another, forgiving each other, just as in Christ God forgave you."

EPHESIANS 4:32

Questions to Ponder

EMPATHY ISN'T SOMETHING THAT COMES EASILY to many of us. But thinking about the life of the person you are trying to forgive can provide a doorway for compassion. See if these questions help you move nearer your goal.

◈ Could you empathize with a pain-giver if you had been in their place?

◈ Does the person who hurt you possess any admirable attributes, or is she unredeemably bad?

✳ What it would cost you to admit that the person who has hurt or disappointed you has some redeeming qualities?

✳ Might admitting such a possibility mean you would have to release a notch of the hostility that has warmed you for so long?

FINDING COMPASSION

WHEN WE CAN FIND THE COMPASSION TO WANT the best for another person, even one it would be easier to hate, we do God's will. He sees what is in our hearts, but it is for us to live the truth. Those of us who know these teachings to be true yet do not live by them, He says, live like the man who built a house on sand. With such unstable foundations, at the first sign of bad weather his house collapsed. Such would happen to us if ours were a faith based on scripture alone. It must be lived and experienced if it is to be relied upon when bad times test us. We have a choice. Live it or lose it.

"If we could read the secret history of our enemies, we should find in each person's life sorrow and suffering enough to disarm all hostility."

HENRY WADSWORTH LONGFELLOW

"Ye have heard that it hath been said, Thou shalt love thy neighbor, and hate thine enemy. But I say unto you, Love your enemies, bless them that curse you, do good to them that hate you, and pray for them which despitefully use you, and persecute you..."

THE GOSPEL OF ST. MATTHEW 5: 43–4

"For if ye love them which love you, what reward have ye? Do not even the publicans the same? And if ye salute your brethren only, what more do ye than others? Do not even the publicans so?"

THE GOSPEL OF ST. MATTHEW 5: 46–47

SEEING OURSELVES IN OTHERS

UNLESS WE FIRST UNDERSTAND THAT THOSE WHO sinned against us are human, just like us (though their past actions may have been evil), and unless we can believe sinners have the capacity to feel regret and a desire to change, we can never truly forgive what they did. It's hard to extend emotions that we can't feel ourselves. The questions set out opposite might help you explore some issues.

Questions to Ponder

❖ Is it hard to believe you are in any sense like those who caused your pain?

❖ Do you feel some acts are unforgivable?

❖ Might it render events a little less painful if you believe sinners are irreversibly evil and essentially different to the rest of us?

❖ Does answering yes to the last question help you deny forgiveness with a clear conscience? If so, you suffer doubly: From the pain of the original wrong and the burden of a frozen future of eternal pain.

EXTENDING UNDERSTANDING

JESUS DISTINGUISHED BETWEEN THE SINNER AND the sin. Behavior stems from character, and character is formed by factors beyond an individual's control. None of us can know the level of blame our tormentors really deserve. It is no excuse, but it can be an explanation if we learn our felon was so badly treated as a child that throughout adult life he chose the kind of oblivion through addictive substances that distorted his moral sense. These adults did not leave their mother's womb that way—they were made so. Though the deeds remain unforgivable, there are no sinners

God would refuse to forgive if their repentance was genuine. We do not hold a lion accountable when survival demands it takes another animal's life. In war, we are told that to kill is just and commendable, and if a loved one dies, the sacrifice is honorable. We are encouraged to feel pride alongside sorrow. The pain of physical and emotional loss is no less; it is simply the interpretation that differs. We often demonize felons to justify why we cannot forgive them. If we do this, we sidestep the painful business of understanding and forgiveness. It is easier to nurse hurt and anger than to free both the sinner and ourselves with forgiveness. In dehumanizing the perpetrator, we continue to deny or ignore our own capacity for evil at the cost of our own absolution. Be aware that this is a tragic position to adopt.

"If we are not to be immobilized by these everyday offences, then we have to forgive each other in order for life to go on...focus not on the act or the trespass, but on the person who committed it, because forgiveness is always of individuals, never of actions. We cannot ever forgive a murder or a theft, but we might learn to forgive a murderer or a thief."

RICHARD HOLLOWAY

"Father, forgive them; for they know not what they do."

THE GOSPEL OF ST. LUKE 23:34

BLESSED IGNORANCE

PUT SIMPLY, IF BY REASON OF IGNORANCE, illness, or innocence a person is unaware of the implications of their actions, they cannot be held accountable in law, and God would forgive them. There must be reciprocal understanding for an emotional event to take place, not because we must be judged worthy by a stern God—God is love—but because anything less than reciprocal understanding and genuine feeling would not convey our sincere expression of forgiveness or acknowledged guilt. Jesus repeatedly taught the values of simplicity, honesty, compassion, faith, and love for one another. Do unto others as you would want done to you, we are taught according to the Gospel of St. Matthew (7:12), but some people have suffered so much that they learned to shut down their feelings to survive, and a learned lack of feeling can lead to violent acts toward others. Such victims may subsequently find it hard to understand that their actions cause pain to others. Empathy or sympathy is no longer in their repertoire of emotions. To judge such a person as you would yourself is inappropriate. We may wish to believe they are like us so we can hate them for their actions, but sympathy might be more appropriate.

SIMPLE RIGHT AND WRONG?

SO HOW DO WE SEPARATE WRONGDOING FROM the wrong doer? Are there ways to recognize that a regrettable act may not have been a deliberate act? And even if it was deliberate at the time, that the perpetrator may have sincerely regretted and repented of that act since? The questions that follow might help you think about how any one person's story is rarely a simple matter of right and wrong, though the same person's acts, taken in isolation, may seem to be.

Questions to Ponder

❖ Before judging someone's actions, can you be certain what he or she intended?

❖ Would you hesitate to judge if the culprit was incapable of being held responsible, for instance, if it was an animal, child, or someone suffering from an illness that left him unaware of the consequences of his action?

❖ Would you feel differently if the act was an accident? Accidents cause regret and grief, but rarely condemnation.

❖ Does considering the exceptions in the last questions start you wondering whether some, if not all, wrongdoers have mitigating circumstances behind their actions?

❖ Imagine yourself living in the shoes of the wrongdoer. Does the misdemeanor become more understandable? Was it prompted by the need for survival rather than wickedness? Could you really hold a lifelong grudge against such a person?

✦ Have you never acted irresponsibly or desperately? Did you never lie to, or cheat your parents, ever? Did you get away with it, or were you found out, but forgiven? None of us immune from foolish actions; unfortunately, sometimes they get out of hand.

✦ Do you want to tie yourself for life to someone else's misjudgment? Jesus teaches us how to behave well for the right reasons, not to gain approval or advantage, but because it aligns us with the will of God.

"A true understanding and humble estimate of oneself is the highest and most valuable of all lessons. To take no account of oneself, but always to think well and highly of others is the highest wisdom and perfection. Should you see another person openly

doing evil, or carrying out a wicked purpose, do not on that account consider yourself better than him, for you cannot tell how long you will remain in a state of grace. We are all frail; consider none more frail than yourself."

THOMAS À KEMPIS

FORGIVING THE PERSON NOT THE DEED

WE DO NOT FORGIVE THE DEED; WE FORGIVE the person who committed the deed. The first step in either offering or accepting forgiveness involves making an honest appraisal of what actually happened. Until you have openly acknowledged the wrong done by others, or by yourself, you cannot begin to forgive, nor to free yourself from the painful feelings you associate with the memory. You cannot change the past, but you can change your emotional response to it. It takes more energy to deny, block, or avoid facing the truth—even more to hold onto anger and the desire for revenge—than it takes to face the facts and deal with them openly. Avoidance and denial is wasted energy. Energy that is no longer available for you to make the most of your present and future, to enjoy what life has yet has to offer you.

"Forgiveness does not change the past, but it does enlarge the future."

PAUL BOESE

FACING THE FACTS

FORGIVENESS IS NOT FORGETTING. YOU MAY never forget the past, nor wish to, but true forgiveness cannot begin until you really face what happened and accept the facts. For as long as you bury your feelings and refuse to examine your past, you will remain locked in a dark room. Only you can decide whether forgiveness—and release—is possible. The questions set out opposite might help you face up to the task ahead.

Questions to Ponder

⟡ Is it hard to forgive because you hold mixed feelings toward the agent of your unhappiness?

⟡ Do you reveal to heal wounds and move on to forgiveness, or do you conceal and allow wounds to fester from fear of the consequences? Only you know if exposure to the truth will cause you and the wrongdoer more pain than good.

⟡ Do you fear exposure, ridicule, or a loss of pride?

FORGIVING AND FORGETTING?

HOW CAN WE FORGIVE WHAT WE CANNOT forget? It is difficult to forgo anger and hurt after fate, neglect, or malicious acts wound us, and no-one should pretend otherwise. Similarly, it is not easy when we feel guilt and shame for wounding others, and wish to be forgiven ourselves. In both cases, quality of life is contaminated by the past and our continued emotional attitude to it. Forgiveness offers a return to sanity. Let God be your support.

"*Whatever a man is unable to correct in himself or in others, he should bear patiently until God ordains otherwise. Consider it is better thus, for the testing of our patience, without which our merits are of little worth. Whenever such obstacles confront you, pray to God that He may grant you His help, and give you grace to endure them in good heart.*"

THOMAS À KEMPIS

RECONCILIATION

RECONCILIATION TAKES TWO. AS WELL AS A wronged person who extends compassionate understanding and freely forgives, there must be someone with a sense of having committed a wrong. We blame parents, teachers, our genetic inheritance, race, color, society, the times we live in—anything rather than take the more courageous and adult step of accepting responsibility for our decisions and actions: I did it, but I am truly sorry and I hope to do better next time. Denial robs victims of a dignified right to feel anger, or to choose to grant forgiveness.

"Forgiveness breaks the chain of causality because he who forgives you out of love takes upon himself the consequences of what you have done. Forgiveness, therefore, always entails a sacrifice."

DAG HAMMARSKJÖLD

UNCONDITIONAL FORGIVENESS

ARCHBISHOP TUTU REMINDS US THAT, AS Christians, we should forgive regardless of whether the wrongdoer is penitent or begs our forgiveness. Christ did not wait for those nailing Him to the cross to ask for His forgiveness; he forgave them anyway. If we have to wait to be asked for forgiveness, we are doubly robbed of control. The offender denies us the freedom to forgive as well as hurting us with the original offence, a double insult. Archbishop Tutu explains God's wisdom in insisting that forgiveness should not be dependent on situations or people. It must be unconditional.

"Jesus did not wait until those who were nailing him to the Cross had asked for forgiveness. He was ready, as they drove in the nails, to pray to his Father to forgive them, and he even provided an excuse for what they were doing. If the victim could forgive only when the culprit confessed, then the victim would be locked into the culprit's whim, locked into victimhood, whatever her own attitude or intention. That would be palpably unjust. In the act of forgiveness we are declaring our faith in the future of a relationship and in the capacity of the wrongdoer to change. ...According to Jesus, we should be ready to do this not just once, not just seven times, but seventytimes seven, without limit."

ARCHBISHOP DESMOND TUTU

MAKING THAT CHOICE

WITH FORGIVENESS COMES CHOICE AND responsibility. You alone can decide if you are able to accept or bestow forgiveness, and you control when and if it is more appropriate to express blame than forgiveness. Each choice has consequences. If you choose to withhold forgiveness for the moment, you must find a positive way to contain your pain, or risk it affecting your health and relationships. Whatever you decide, there will be times when it is good to release the energy usually spent on restraining anger. Anger is a survival tool, like mankind's innate caution with heights and fear of death. Life is 5 percent what happens to you and 95 percent what you make of what happens to you. You have choice at all times. Bad and sad things happen to everyone, but whether you let them color your whole life or just add shade and contour to it is up to you. Holding on to anguish does nothing to alter material facts or bring back a time past. It does do a huge amount to ruin your present, and all those presents make up your future. Forgiveness is a decision you are free to make. Some make it early, some late, some not at all; but it is in the gift of each one of us.

FORGIVENESS FOREVER

FORGIVENESS IS AN ONGOING SPIRITUAL practice; it is not a single act. It is not to be accomplished in an afternoon, unless the offence was very minor and fairly recent. Older, deeper wounds are, of course, the hardest to forgive. When we are adult and have allowed a wound to fester, perhaps since childhood, it will be harder to heal than if we had attended to it immediately. Even more difficult to heal are wounds that were repeated often over time until our reactions became dulled, and our appropriate angry responses were buried deep within us. Forgiveness of such major hurts cannot be achieved in a moment's well-intended or insincere absolution. Forgiveness requires a generous and sincere change of heart, a profound alteration in attitude and beliefs that demands a sustained effort and sometimes the support of others, whether professional healthcare workers, fellow church-members, or our cherished friends.

PRAYERS, POEMS,

and

THOUGHTS

of

FORGIVENESS

"I offer up unto Thee my prayers and intercessions, for those especially who have in any matter hurt, grieved, or found fault with me, or who have done me any damage or displeasure.
For all those also whom, at any time, I have vexed, troubled, burdened, and scandalized, by words or deeds, knowingly or in ignorance: that Thou wouldst grant us all equally pardon for our sins, and for our offences against each other. Amen."

THOMAS A KEMPIS

"Oh Divine Master,
Grant that I may not so much seek
To be consoled as to console,
To be understood as to understand,
To be loved as to love,
For it is in giving that we receive,
It is in pardoning that we are pardoned
And it is in dying that we are born
To eternal life."

ST. FRANCIS OF ASSISI

*"As the first martyr Stephen prayed
to thee for his murderers, O Lord, so
we fall before thee and pray: forgive
all who hate and maltreat us and let
not one of them perish because of us,
but may all be saved by thy grace,
O God the all-bountiful."*

ORTHODOX CHRISTIAN PRAYER

"We are all capable of good and evil. We are not born bad: everybody has something good inside. Some hide it, some neglect it. But it is there. God created us to love and to be loved, so it is our test from God to choose one path or another."

MOTHER TERESA

"*Forgiving and being reconciled to our enemies or our loved ones is not about pretending that things are other than they are. it is not about patting one another on the back and turning a blind eye to the wrong. True reconciliation exposes the awfulness, the abuse, the pain, the hurt, the truth. It could even sometimes make things worse. It is a risky undertaking, but in the end it is worthwhile, because in the end dealing with the real situation helps to bring real healing. Superficial reconciliation can bring only superficial healing."*

ARCHBISHOP DESMOND TUTU

"Therefore I say unto you,
What things soever ye desire, when ye
pray, believe that ye receive them,
and ye shall have them.
And when ye stand praying, forgive,
if ye have ought against any: that
your Father also which is in heaven
may forgive you your trespasses.
But if ye do not forgive, neither will
your Father which is in heaven
forgive your trespasses."

THE GOSPEL OF ST. MARK 11: 24–26

"I sought my God,
my God I could not see;
I sought my soul, my soul eluded me;
I sought my brother,
and I found all three."

ANON.

PART 6

When Forgiving Seems Difficult

THE BIGGER THE GRIEVANCE, THE harder it may be to make the decision to forgive or to blame the person you hold responsible. As Christians, we are commanded to forgive others if we hope to find forgiveness ourselves, yet, after a traumatic event, feelings of confusion and turmoil may be so strong that for a time, perhaps always, honest compliance with this Christian principle will be difficult, if not impossible. Here are ways to help you through that maze.

WHY SHOULD I ABSOLVE
THE GUILTY?

YOU MAY ASK WHY SOMEONE WHO HAS CAUSED so much pain should be released from responsibility and accountability by your forgiveness? We all nurse the unrealistic wish that life should be fair. Holding a grudge at least gives us a feeling of control and a sense of moral superiority. But those who expend energy in hating are the ones who suffer most. Your pain doesn't hurt the person you resent. In fact, continued anguish could increase the satisfaction given to a disturbed mind. For as long as you nurse a grievance, you are the one imprisoned—by your inability to let go of the bitterness—while the person who caused you hurt remains emotionally free. Every time we experience such pain, we hold ourselves apart from God and our fellow human beings. If we can remember the huge debt we owe to our heavenly Father, who has forgiven us our sins countless times, we may find it in our hearts to forgive others. If we cannot, we turn away from Him.

WHEN IT'S HARD TO FORGIVE

IF YOU CANNOT FORGIVE JUST YET, HAVE SOME compassion for yourself and the suffering you continue to bear. Your feelings at this moment are valid and your decision is right for you right now. The thoughts set out opposite might help you come to terms with some of the issues you face.

THOUGHTS TO PONDER

⬧ Recognize that sin is just one of the many potential expressions of a human being. We recognize it because, to some degree, we exhibit it. To begin to forgive it helps if you can recognize your shared humanity with the wrongdoer.

⬧ If you demonize the sinner, you place him or her outside the realm of influence, regret and change, and remove yourself from all hope of release from pain.

FORGIVING ENEMIES

CHRIST SET THE EXAMPLE OF FORGIVING ONE'S enemies. Most difficult to forgive are those who wound others, physically or emotionally, and have no regret. Can we find a way to forgive even "the unforgivable?" As the philosopher Jacques Derrida accurately identifies, only the unforgivable need our forgiveness. The repentant have already returned to the flock, and are thus forgivable and forgiven. Jesus's teaching attracted the most difficult social cases, but he rejected no one and forgave all when hearts were sincere and faith in redemption strong. Can we emulate his example?

"*There is only forgiveness, if there is any,
where there is the unforgivable.*"

JACQUES DERRIDA

"*Doing an injury puts you
below your enemy;
Revenging one makes you but
even with him;
Forgiving it sets you above him.*"

BENJAMIN FRANKLIN

"God's love for us and our love for others is the single greatest motivating force in the world. And this love and the good it creates will always triumph over hatred and evil. But if you are to be true partners with God in

the transfiguration of his world and help bring this triumph of love over hatred, of good over evil, you must begin by understanding that as much as God loves you, God equally loves your enemies."

ARCHBISHOP DESMOND TUTU
WITH DOUGLAS ABRAMS

IS ANY ACT UNFORGIVABLE?

SOME SINS MAY BE SO ENORMOUS AS TO SEEM unforgivable (to us, if not to God), even when the perpetrator is penitent. To say an act is completely unforgivable separates it from the humans who caused it and experienced it. If we remain unable to forgive the enormity of a crime, we treat the perpetrator as if he or she were somehow different from us; not a fellow human being subject to lapses, failure, misguided beliefs, and bizarre reasons for behavior. The criminal may or may not be forgiven by the victim, depending on whether the actor can be distinguished from the act, but the act remains evil and will always be remembered as such. What forgiveness gives us is a harmonious way to remember and to honor past pain while moving on into the future and a new life.

"...people have done such awful things and yet it would appear that in so many ways, they are just like the rest of us: they are in other respects 'normal.'
... human beings—and that means human beings in general—are capable of great evil and of great good."

HANNAH ARENDT

PARABLE

Reconciliation in South Africa

Archbishop Desmond Tutu recounts a tale that can help us understand the nature of forgiveness when it relates to acts that might be beyond bearing. He tells the story of a lady who came before the South African Truth Commission and stated, simply, "A commission or a government cannot forgive. Only I, eventually, could do it. (And I am not ready to forgive.)" Until we are able to separate the sin from the sinner, he explains, we cannot truly forgive or know how we are forgiven. We are free to choose to hold onto bitterness and a desire for retribution instead of forgiveness. It is a matter of grace if and when we can reach the Christian understanding that will release us. We, the victims of great sins, are deserving of compassion in the meantime.

DOES FORGIVING CONDONE EVIL?

WHEN AN ACT IS SO HORRIFIC IT BECOMES unforgivable—and, in some cases, when forgiveness seems just too enormous and overwhelming a proposition, we should leave matters in God's capable hands. It may seem that if we humans were to forgive, we could be accused of condoning the evil that has been perpetrated. On the contrary, forgiveness starts from the recognition that a wrong has been committed. Forgiveness in no way excuses or belittles the horror of the act. But if we do choose to forgive, we need not forget. As individuals and as a society we need to learn from evil acts if we are to prevent their repetition in another place and time in the future. Atrocities must never be swept under the carpet, regardless of whether we forgive those who perpetrated them or not. Forgiving is not forgetting.

"In spite of everything, I still believe people are really good at heart."

ANNE FRANK

ACTS THAT SHAKE YOUR FAITH

MAYBE IT IS GOD YOU NEED TO FORGIVE. SOME acts and experiences shake our faith to the point that we need to express anger at the core of our belief. How can an all-knowing God allow bad things to happen to good people? Maybe your faith has been disturbed by a death that deprives you of companionship, support, and a secure lifestyle? To rail against the dead may seem shameful, but is far from unusual and, in the expression of honest anguish, is a healthy, reasonable reaction. Don't worry. Our dead knew us well enough to understand our anger if we knew them well.

"Genuine forgiveness does not deny anger but faces it head-on."

ALICE MILLER

"Grant that some acts are utterly inexcusable and profoundly wrong. Grant that such acts are monstrous, brutal, gross, horrifying, and atrocious. Grant that such acts should never be excused justified or condoned. Grant that we should forever decry their immorality and that their heinous nature should be recorded in human history never to be erased. Grant that victims should be honored in memory and survivors respected. What does all this imply about the forgiveability or

unforgivability of the perpetrators of those acts? Whatever they have done, and however much we may be tempted to refer to them as "monsters," "madmen," or "rotten," the fundamental fact remains: perpetrators are human beings and our fellow creatures. They are persons with a capacity for moral reflection and transformation, and we should treat them accordingly ... it is persons, not deeds, whom others will avoid or confront, and in the end, forgive or not forgive."

TRUDY GOVIER

IS CHRISTIAN FORGIVENESS CONDITIONAL?

THE COMMAND TO CONFESS OUR FAILINGS AND extend our forgiveness might suggest God's forgiveness is conditional. How can this be when the gospels tell us we shall be forgiven more than seven times seventy—an ancient way of suggesting a number beyond measure? We are also told that we can expect to be forgiven as a father forgives his child—unconditionally. So how can there be preconditions? The apparent paradox of a divine forgiveness that is at once limited and unlimited is resolved in the Bible: forgiveness is an aspect of God's grace, and as such, is beyond limit, definition, or quantification; and yet the forgiveness He extends to us is not to be demanded as a right and is not without cost. These are the conditions. And when we are sincerely repentant, there are no limits to what may be forgiven.

"Those who are well have no need of a
physician, but those who are sick;
I came not to call the righteous,
but sinners [to repentance]."

LUKE 5:31–2

PRAYERS, POEMS,

and

THOUGHTS

of

FORGIVENESS

"In your great love, O God, pardon our sins and restore a right spirit in our hearts. Guide us to love you with our whole being, so that our actions toward others might magnify you and that all may come to know grace upon grace as promised in your Word. Amen."

METHODIST PRAYER

"Our Father,
forgive all our misdeeds
and wipe away our sin,
for you are great and compassionate;
your mercy knows no bounds.
My heart lies before you, O my God.
Look deep within it.
See these memories of mine,
for you are my hope."

ST. AUGUSTINE

"There are people in South Africa who have committed the most unbelievable atrocities... However, monstrous deeds do not turn the perpetrators into monsters. A human person does not ultimately lose his or her humanity, which is characterized by the divine image in which every individual is created... The premise underlying this

. . . is that it is possible for people to change, insofar as perpetrators can come to realize the evil of their actions and even be able to plead for the forgiveness of those they have wronged . . . the scales can fall from the eyes of those who believed firmly in apartheid, and they can in fact see that what they believed was wrong." ARCHBISHOP DESMOND TUTU

"O, Lamb of God that taketh away the sins of the world have mercy upon us, O, Lamb of God that taketh away the sins of the world have mercy upon us, O, Lamb of God that taketh away the sins of the world give us Thy Peace. Amen."

ANGLICAN PRAYER

"Tend Your sick one, O Lord Christ.
Rest Your weary ones.
Bless Your dying ones,
Soothe Your suffering ones,
Pity Your afflicted ones,
Shield Your joyous ones,
And all for Your love's sake. Amen."

ST. AUGUSTINE

"When we love we want to forgive. It is so with God. Remember the tax gatherer (Luke 18) at the back of the Temple not daring to raise his eyes, in contrast to the Pharisee who prayed at the front, boasting of his accomplishments. It was not he who was justified, but the tax gatherer who prayed:

'Lord be merciful to me a sinner.' that is a most marvellous prayer. Who, praying that, can fail to hear in his or her heart those words of our Lord on the cross: 'Father, forgive them, they know not what they do.' It is beautiful to receive God's forgiveness, and it is there for the taking."

CARDINAL BASIL HUME

PART 7

Getting Over Resentment, Rage, and Revenge

THE ABILITY TO FORGIVE REPRESENTS the only sane and Christian way forward, but may be unattainable—just yet… Anger, resentment, and the wish to exact revenge may be preventing you from moving forward. The thoughts and exercises on the following pages may help.

RESENTMENT

ANGER AND RESENTMENT ARE A COMMON REASON for remaining unable to contemplate forgiveness. When we have been badly hurt or deceived, justifiable rage may seem to be our only option when we feel powerless yet have the urge to do something. But it is exhausting to hold onto feelings of anger and hatred. It demands an obsessive focus of pent-up energy. Contained rage is always preferable to retaliation—that would be game over—but an offender is unlikely to be affected by our angry feelings in any way. So we suffer twice over, and they go free. Being aware of this can feed a spiral of anger: Watch how your feelings tighten up another notch when you think about the injustice, unless you are so foolish as to choose to let out the anger in an act of retaliation. Then the offender has really won. You have become no better than him. The ability to forgive represents the only sane and Christian way forward, even if it remains unattainable just yet.

> *"Resentment is a poison one takes
> hoping to harm another."*
>
> ANON

GETTING OVER RESENTMENT

REFUSE TO ALLOW PAINFUL REACTIONS TO continue to possess you. The focused obsessions of love and hate are similar. And it is as easy to fall out of hate as it is to fall out of love. If there are scores to be settled, know that it is not your task to settle them. Surrendering your anger may be the hardest thing in the world to contemplate, perhaps, but it will be the easiest choice to live with once accomplished. Why hold onto bitterness in the present for something that is no longer occurring? Reclaim control and you release yourself from bondage to past hurts. The forgiver gains more than the forgiven, without a doubt, but as with all acts of charity, your motivation in extending forgiveness should be selfless if it is to be genuine.

"Without forgiveness life is governed by an endless cycle of resentment and retaliation"

ROBERTO ASSAGIOLI

I'M TOO ANGRY TO FORGIVE

AFTER YEARS OF PAIN AND ANGUISH WE CAN become so tightly bound to rage that we would not know any other way to be. To be free of anger would mean a change of identity that is too frightening to contemplate. We can forget who we were before the anger. Your potential for happiness remains intact under all the layers of angry defense, perhaps if accessible only after support and counseling, but it will still be there. The road that was closed when you were traumatized can be reopened. Your onward journey may, neces- sarily, be a little different than you had anticipated, but the barriers you had to erect can finally come down. To forgive does involve a degree of compassion and understanding for the perpetrator that you may fear will rob you of your moral indignation and a right to rage. When you are feeling helpless and out of control, understanding and compassion can be welcome substitute emotions. But they can seem too much to ask when you have already given too much. This is not as it seems. Compassion and forgiveness always benefit the giver more than the given. It is you who carry a pain that can be released. Think about that. The offender was never touched by the burden of corrosive hatred you bear. He will always be responsible for what he did and will answer to God.

"True forgiveness is a willingness to change your mind about your Self."

ROBERT HOLDEN

"Yet Man is born into trouble, as the sparks fly upward."

JOB 5:7

LOOKING AT YOUR ANGER

IF YOU HONESTLY EXAMINE YOUR FEELINGS OF anger you may discover that they mask deeper feelings. If you rage at someone, is it really the result of a prior aggravation you have suffered that you pass on now because it remains alive in you? The more often you deny your real feelings, the more you become like Gulliver captured by the Lilliputians in Jonathan Swift's novel, tied by a million little restraints. With each denial you move further and further away from your true being and all that you might be. Let the questions set out opposite start you thinking.

Questions to Ponder

❖ Is your anger tainted by shame, guilt, or self-blame for the situation or person who caused you to experience these feelings?

❖ Do you feel betrayed by any dishonor and lack of respect shown to you?

❖ Is there grief within your anger for a loss you were unable to prevent, or for being deserted, perhaps?

❖ Is your anger tinged with helplessness, a reminder that a sense of control is always illusory?

IDENTIFYING YOUR
ANGER TRIGGERS

TO BE AWARE HOW YOUR ANGER STARTS IS TO know where and how to put on the brakes. When you can see it arrive and leave, you can develop strategies to control it rather than be controlled by it. Those who live around you will be spared some of the fallout they suffer from living next to a volcano! Are you patient in a queue, for example, or do you seethe when made to wait? Can you observe the bad driving of another driver without being personally slighted? Do you argue with the television and with newspapers? Write a list of things that trigger your rage.

ANGER-MANAGEMENT TIPS

◈ Ask a friend or family member to tell you what they think annoys you. They surely know because they have learned to avoid those topics.

◈ Be willing to listen to what they tell you without proving them right!

LOOKING FOR PATTERNS

GET TO KNOW YOUR ANGER IN AN OBJECTIVE way, as the unwelcome visitor it is, by looking for patterns in situations that inflame your anger. Do you recognize similar attitudes in those who reared or taught you? Are these attitudes truly yours? Think about them by using some or all of the prompt questions set out opposite.

Questions to Ponder

✤ Is it more important for you to win over another person than to feel you are, and always were, free?

✤ Why do you think this is?

✤ When did you acquire this belief?

✤ Has it served you well?

✤ Have you had problems communicating with someone in your past?

TAKE A BREAK

NEXT TIME YOU FEEL THE RAGE RISING INSIDE, and forgiveness remains too high a mountain to climb, try to take a moment to imagine yourself in the other person's position before you lose control. Do you remember the characters in Charles Kingsley's children's story, *The Water Babies*? There was a Mrs-Do-As-You-Would-Be-Done-By, whose behavior was, as her name suggests, exemplary; and her opposite number, Mrs-Done-By-As-You-Did, a far more alarming character who catered for the willfully misbehaved. Children who read the tale were made aware that there will be, at some point, a reckoning for the ways in which we choose to behave. Which character's attention do you think your behavior might attract right now?

> *"You attract what you believe you deserve."*
> ROBERT HOLDEN

POSITIVE WAYS TO RELEASE ANGER

IF THE PROSPECT OF RELEASING ALL YOUR anger is too frightening to contemplate, learn how to let it out in a more measured and controlled fashion. It is a mistake to believe all anger is bad. The spiritually developed person is one who knows and accepts all that he or she may be—including angry when the occasion demands it. Jesus threw out the moneylenders from the temple; he did not petition them to leave. A spiritual quality is brought to bear when you know how to use your anger with discrimination. Enough, and no more. If you are under real and immediate physical threat for example, or if you see an act of cruelty to another when you can safely make a difference, be enlivened by your anger. You might use it in the service of a political cause, to empower a creative endeavor, to rescue a person in danger, when you need to run the fastest mile, and so on. Always find ways to express your anger and rage that will not cause harm to others, even those to whom you believe vengeance is due. I am not suggesting you should repress or deny your honest feelings of rage or shame, just use them creatively rather than negatively if at all possible because bottling up anger does not always enhance creativity. It may deaden your responses to life. If this describes you, then extending forgiveness can be a means to releasing a tidal wave of blocked creativity.

WAYS TO CHANNEL RAGE

◈ Let it all out through art or writing.

◈ Try sporting activities or other physical labor of some kind.

◈ Spring clean the house or dig the garden.

◈ Use this channeling activity to count to three, metaphorically speaking. Permit honest feelings to well up and be lived through, but in a contained environment that does not extend the problems you have to deal with.

SUPERNATURAL POWERS

DO YOU RECALL THE NEWS STORY OF A WOMAN who lifted a car to rescue a child beneath it? Asked by journalists to repeat the feat when not fired by need, she could not lift the same car. Once you know your pain and how to contain it appropriately, you have access to a major energy conduit, instead of a messy, spluttering fissure. This can be your powerhouse, providing the effort of keeping a lid on your anger until you need it does not consume all your energy, and so long as it does not affect the innocent when they accidentally disturb the lid.

GETTING OVER THE ANGER

AT THE END OF THE DAY, IS YOUR ANGER worthwhile; is it making a difference to anyone but you, and are the personal costs and effort you expend in controlling (or not controlling) it worth it? These considerations may be of greater relevance than your ability to forgive according to prescribed religious or social ideals. If you find it really difficult to let go of anger—perhaps if it has become self-defining and to drop it might threaten your very identity—start by pretending. As we do, so we become. Fake it until it you make it. Most learning happens that way. You had to learn to ride a bicycle and even to walk by feigning confidence, suffering a few spills along the way until you really could do it. Have sincere intention and be prepared for a few accidents, but make a start today.

"To err is human, to forgive divine."
ALEXANDER POPE

I'M TOO HURT TO FORGIVE

THE EVENT THAT CAUSED YOUR PAIN IS OVER, even though its consequences may remain with you for the rest of your life. The sooner you release your attachment to your negative memories, the sooner you can recover and rebuild your life. You are much greater than your pain. If the memory is so painful that you deny what happened, you cut yourself off from your real nature and deplete your energy. Repeated in enough areas of experience, this leads to alienation and a loss of purpose. If, however, you learn from weaknesses and mistakes, you grow beyond them.

"Everything is God's to give and to take away, so share what you've been given, and that includes yourself."

MOTHER TERESA

EXPRESSING THE PAIN

AN EFFECTIVE PRACTICAL WAY TO START TO tackle some of the hurt is to write a letter to the wrongdoer. Whether the individual ever receives the document is a matter for you to decide. In most cases it might be better that the letter remains unsent, because, inevitably, it expresses your experience, not gold-plated truth. What is important is that you openly admit to yourself in the writing all the feelings you have nursed and suppressed since the event. If the person addressed has died and you know of their burial site, you may gain resolution from reading your letter to him or her at the graveside. If you want to send the letter, be aware that what you write could be read by other eyes and might cause unjustified hurt or upset to innocent parties. Also be mindful of what you send being considered libellous.

"You can't undo anything you've already done, but you can face up to it. You can tell the truth. You can seek forgiveness. And then let God do the rest."

ANON

WHEN IT'S TOO MUCH TO BEAR

IF YOUR WOUNDS ARE SO GREAT OR PROBLEMS too overwhelming for you to handle alone, be guided by your instinct and seek confidential moral and legal professional support. Search out the support of a friend, a family member, or church official, perhaps; one in whom you can place complete trust. Some dilemmas need professional help to start disentangling. What might be impossibly difficult for us everyday people to make sense of is daily fare for psychotherapists, who tread cautiously and make no global recommendations regarding the wisdom of forgiveness. Instead, they suggest each case proceeds according to the history and capacity of the wounded individual. In certain circumstances, to attempt forgiveness at the cost of self-respect and personal truth would be ill-advised. Forgiveness requires understanding and empathy if it is to be genuine, and, if the hurt is great, it may take time, guidance, and exploration in a therapeutic environment.

PAIN FROM THE PAST

HURT MAY BE ASSOCIATED WITH ACTS THAT TOOK place before your birth. Collective negativity around the history of a family, race, faith, or country extends far beyond your immediate or personal experience. Indeed, it may seem disloyal to our very identity even to consider forgiveness. But this misconstrues the meaning of forgiveness. We only forgive where wrong has been committed and blame is deserved. Forgiveness follows evil or error, not accident or misfortune (which might be salved with an excuse or apology). Those events took place in the past, perhaps long ago. Your scenario has been rolling out daily ever since. We are not bound to repeat our suffering, or that of our parents, race or nation. Gain solace from the knowledge that it is possible to think and behave with God as our witness, not man.

"Forgiveness is the fragrance that the violet sheds on the heel that has crushed it."

RUSSIAN PROVERB

FREED FROM THE MEMORY

FORGIVING IN NO SENSE CONDONES WRONGDOING and never makes valid such behavior in the future. What it does do is allows us to admit what happened and how we feel about it, and permits us to forgive ourselves for having been powerless to change what happened. We need to hold onto what the experience has taught us, but freed from the pain associated with the memory. Only when we have forgiven ourselves can we really hope to forgive others involved and free ourselves of the burden we carry. We cannot turn back the clock and have things be other than they were. What we can do is free ourselves from the resentment, pain, or anger we have held since and move into a clearer future.

"The sun, though it passes through dirty places, yet remains as pure as before."

FRANCIS BACON

I'M TOO LOYAL TO FORGIVE

FEAR OF DISLOYALTY CAN BE A STRONG BARRIER to forgiveness. We may feel we owe it to another person not to forgive a wrongdoer. We may even feel we must exact vengeance on another's behalf, particularly if the victim is unable to seek redress in person. This often occurs when we wish to protect and honor someone now deceased. If the departed is not here to tell us that this is or is not necessary, or, more likely, to tell us to let go and move on in life, we can become trapped by this emotionally charged loyalty. Any act of forgiveness could seem like an act of betrayal. You may forgive and still choose not to reconcile with the individuals you have forgiven. Whether or not you wish them to be a part of your future life is an entirely separate decision. What you can do is let them go from your emotional life in the present, and, by the act of forgiving them and yourself, lay the ghost of your factual past.

> *"We win by tenderness. We conquer by forgiveness."*
>
> FREDERICK W. ROBERTSON

THINKING ABOUT NON-RETALIATION

DO YOU HOLD THE BELIEF THAT ONLY THE WEAK forgive; strong people retaliate? Where did you first learn that? It's often easier to blame than to forgo retaliation and forgive. After all, many people would understand your motives for revenge, while compassion might take more explaining. Answer the questions set out opposite to start thinking about your personal style of dealing with guilt and blame.

Questions to Ponder

❖ Have you ever needed to be forgiven?

❖ How good are you at accepting blame when you have made a mistake?

❖ Is there always a 'but…' in your case, while others are clearly to be blamed?

❖ Do you dwell on the person you blame a lot of the time?

❖ Do you tend toward passive aggression, always muttering, gossiping, and finding fault with events and people?

RETALIATION BUSTING

❖ Try changing the thought whenever the "guilty" person or painful incident enters your mind. "Switch channels" by thinking of someone else or another topic.

❖ Have you ever tried to see the good in people? Try to curb your aggression for one whole day and see how it feels.

❖ Resist the urge to retaliate when you feel provoked. Instead make only affirmative and positive responses. Do you find people react differently than usual to you? How does that make you feel?

❖ As you choose which channels you play in your head, ask yourself why you are choosing to play the more painful one?

"If you are patient in one moment of anger, you will escape a hundred days of sorrow."

CHINESE PROVERB

TURNING THE OTHER CHEEK

JESUS' TEACHING WENT FURTHER THAN THE dual concepts of win or lose. He taught that we should not resist evil, but by acceptance of God's will, disarm it; so that if we are hit on one cheek we should offer the other for the same treatment; and if we are robbed of our coat, we should practice generosity and insist they take our cloak too. These injunctions marked a radical departure from the Old Testament laws that had demanded retaliation: an eye for an eye, a tooth for a tooth. It takes a brave and trusting person to practice non-retaliation under threat, but Jesus tells us that if we want to accept God as our Lord, and we would be as His children, we must accept that He is Lord of all—of the sinner as well as the sinned against—and act accordingly. This is amongst the most challenging of Jesus' teachings.

STILL LONGING FOR REVENGE?

IF YOU STILL FEEL YOU NEED VENGEANCE, TRY to weigh up why, and what good it would serve. Be sure of your motive. A more constructive approach is to change the way you view the situation. Take a different slant on it. There follow on pages 280–81 some hidden motives to get you thinking. When you give in to thoughts of revenge you actually expand the original hurt. It is your rage that keeps your pain, and its cause, ever present in your life. You have chosen to eat, sleep, and walk with this offender every day of your life by rousing your hatred for him or her. There is as much intimacy in hatred as in loving. In both cases our focus seldom wavers. It can be easier to continue to lash out than to revise what you believe, with the risk that others may call you weak or foolish, or worse, if you forgive instead. There is no loss in what is freely given. The offender has not scored another victory if you realize you can forgive him. Peace and serenity can be yours again even if it has been a long time since you misplaced them. Forgive or seek forgiveness if you can. Forgiveness, practiced daily, brings harmony to your life and that of the people around you.

Questions to Ponder

❖ Does raging at others mask a fear of owning up to some responsibility a little nearer to home?

❖ Would retaliation in any way alter the past?

❖ Would the proof that you can also act irresponsibly advance your case against the original offender?

✦ Are you really seeking to restore your sense of power, and with it the more comfortable illusion of thinking you are in control? In this you were hopelessly seeking to restore what no human being ever had.

"How much more grievous are the consequences of anger than the causes of it."

MARCUS AURELIUS

"He who seeks revenge should dig two graves."

CHINESE PROVERB

"For he maketh the sun to rise on the evil and the good, and sendeth rain on the just and on the unjust."

THE GOSPEL OF ST. MATTHEW 5:45

CHOOSING THE RIGHT PATH

IF YOU CANNOT FORGIVE, YOU HAVE CHOSEN TO nurse your anger and keep the pain alive when it could be otherwise. Regret and disappointment keeps you ensnared and prevents you from realizing your potential for happiness now. Maybe you feel the best part of you was destroyed or taken from you. There is so much more to who you are, what you can do, and where you can find joy. Do not tie yourself to the one person or thing that did not turn out as you hoped. You can choose to perpetuate the misery, or move away from it and allow the past to rest in peace.

"Forgiveness is not an occasional act:
it is an attitude."

MARTIN LUTHER KING, JR.

AFTER FORGIVENESS

FORGIVENESS HAS TO BE CONSTANTLY RENEWED and genuinely heartfelt, but when we truly forgive, we reach an understanding that allows us to forgo anger and grief. We are ready to let go of the past, despite its painful memories, not the actual memories. After forgiveness, memories remain, but we do not dwell on them obsessively. The emotional undertow is lessened and brought within our control—most of the time, at least. We accept that the secret hopes for more positive outcomes we cherished have come to naught. We also accept, however reluctantly, that we cannot change the past, and are now willing to move on with life, despite the painful memories. Our future will inevitably include this unwanted taint, but through forgiveness of the wrongdoer, and of ourselves, we are able to love and laugh again. We choose to embrace the present, to move on to whatever new experiences life has in store, and to face the future broadened by the experiences we have survived.

MARTIN LUTHER KING, JR.

POEMS, PRAYERS,

and

THOUGHTS

of

FORGIVENESS

"Strange that so much suffering is caused because of the misunderstandings of God's true nature. God's heart is more gentle than the Virgin's first kiss upon the Christ. And God's forgiveness to all, to any thought or act, is more certain than our own being."

ST. CATHERINE OF SIENNA

*"Lord Jesus, you were called the
friend of sinners, be my friend, for
I acknowledge that I have sinned.
Forgive the wrong that I have done
and the right that I have failed to do; my
secret and my more open sins; my sins of
ignorance and my deliberate sins; sins to
please myself and sins to please others;
the sins which I remember, and the sins
which I have forgotten; forgive all these,
for it was for me also that you died.
My Lord and Saviour. Amen."*

JOHN WESLEY

"O Lord Jesus, because, being full of foolishness, we often sin and have to ask pardon, help us to forgive as we would be forgiven, mentioning neither old offences against us, nor dwelling on them in thought, nor being influenced by them in heart, but loving each other freely, as thou freely loved us; for thy name's sake. Amen."

CHRISTINA ROSSETTI

"I seem forsaken and alone,
I hear the lion roar,
And every door is shut but one,
And that is Mercy's door."

WILLIAM COWPER

"His heart was as great as the world but there was no room in it to hold the memory of a wrong."

RALPH WALDO EMERSON

"The quality of mercy is not strained,
It droppeth as the gentle rain from heaven
Upon the place beneath:
it is twice blessed;
It blesseth him that gives,
and him that takes."

FROM THE MERCHANT OF VENICE
BY WILLIAM SHAKESPEARE

"And blessed be the King, who hath forgiven ❖ My wickedness to him, and left me hope ❖ That in mine own heart I can live down sin ❖ And be his mate hereafter in the heavens ❖ Before high God."

ALFRED, LORD TENNYSON

"Blessed is he whose transgression is forgiven, whose sin is covered. Blessed is the man unto whom the Lord imputeth not iniquity, and in whose spirit there is no guile."

PSALM 32

"Know all and you will pardon all."

THOMAS À KEMPIS

"If we could read the secret history of our enemies, we should find in each persons life sorrow and suffering enough to disarm all hostility."

HENRY WADSWORTH LONGFELLOW

"Brothers in humanity who live after us, let not your hearts be hardened against us, for, if you take pity on us poor ones, God will be more likely to have mercy on you. But pray God that he may be willing to absolve us all."

FRANÇOIS VILLON

*"Bless the Lord, O my soul, and forget
not all his benefits:
Who forgiveth all thine iniquities; who
healeth all thy diseases;
Who redeemeth thy life from destruction;
who crowneth thee with loving kindness
and tender mercies;
Who satisfieth thy mouth with good
things; so that thy youth is renewed like
the eagle's."*

PSALM 103:2–5

BIBLIOGRAPHY

All Bible quotes are taken from the King James Version.

Forgiveness and Revenge by Trudy Govier, Routledge 2002.

God Has a Dream: a vision of hope for our time by Desmond Tutu with Douglas Abrams, Doubleday 2004.

Hannah Arendt: Eichmann in Jerusalem by Julia Kristeva, Columbia University Press 2001.

On Cosmopolitanism and Forgiveness by Jacques Derrida, Routledge 2001.

On Forgiveness—how can we forgive the unforgivable? by Richard Holloway, Canongate 2002.

Penguin Books: Great Ideas. The Inner Life, Penguin Classics 2004.

The Book of Peace: finding the spirit in a busy world by Mother Teresa, excerpted from *A Simple Path* compiled by Lucinda Vardey, Rider 1996.

The Mystery of Love by Cardinal Basil Hume, Darton, Longman and Todd 2004.

Yes, There is Something You Can Do. 150 Prayers, Poems, and Meditations for Times of Need compiled by Jamie C. Miller, Fair Winds Press 2003.